FINDING ZEN IN COW TOWN

30 POEMS ABOUT KANSAS CITY

FINDING ZEN IN COW TOWN

30 POEMS ABOUT KANSAS CITY

Edited by Jason Ryberg and Jeanette Powers

Kansas City Spartan Missouri
Press

Spartan Press
Kansas City, Missouri
spartanpresskc.com

Copyright (c) Spartan Press 2017
First Edition 1 3 5 7 9 10 8 6 4 2
ISBN: 978-1-946642-11-0
LCCN: 2017931607

Design, edits and layout: Jason Ryberg, Ezhno Martin, Jeanette Powers
Cover and interior photos: Jon Bidwell
All rights reserved. No part of this publication may be reproduced or transmitted in any form or by any means, electronic or mechanical, including photocopying, recording or by info retrieval system, without prior written permission from the author.

ACKNOWLEDGMENTS

Prospero's Books and Spartan Press would like to thank Jeanette Powers, j. d. tulloch, Jason Preu, M. Scott Douglass, Shawn Pavey, Shaun Saving, Jesse Kates, Jim Holroyd, Steven H.Bridgens, Thomas Mason, Beth Dille, Ezhno Martin, Mason Wolf, Katherine Samet, The Osage Arts Community, The West Plaza Tomato Co. and The Robert J. Deuser Foundation For Libertarian Studies.

CONTENTS

Finding Zen in Cow Town / Shawn Pavey / 1
It's a Food Town / Jose Faus / 3
Kansas City / Fredric Sims / 4
Muehlebach Hotel, Kansas City / Denise Low / 7
Driving Through Kansas
   in Late Autumn / Phil Miller / 8
Kansas City Renga / Silvia Kofler / 9
davey's stagecoach / Sharon Eiker / 10
the cowboys got anchored here
   by demonic forces / Ezhno Martin / 11
Expelled Prophets: A Never City / Crista Siglin / 12
Jackson County Baby / Jeanette Powers / 14
UNTITLED #3 / Brandon Whitehead / 15
Kansas City / Xanath Caraza / 17
A Barbequed Life (1967) / Stanley E. Banks / 21
No Blue Mondays, No Smoky Horns / Steve Bridgens / 23
Attention: Oak Street Residents / Gustavo Adolfo Aybar / 24
untitled k.c. poem / Jacob Johanson / 25
Broadway Street / Victor Clevenger / 27
The Benefits of Age / John Dorsey / 29
Saturday Night At Longview Lake, Disguised
   As Purgatory Cove / John Mark Eberhart / 30
Summer Magic / Joseph Davis / 32
Deep Chigger Shade / W. E. Leathem / 34
Surrogate City / Huascar Medina / 36

Kansas City: After Filming, Robert Altman's
  Musicians Stop by the Club / Kevin Rabas / 37
Revival / Glenn North / 38
Kansas City Nights / William Peck / 41
james street 3 a.m. (or, view
  from the roof of a '57 ford) / Victor Smith / 44
The War Goes Ever On From The City
  Where It Began / Jason Preu / 45
What's Up Kansas City? / Serenity / 47
Scenes From 39th St. Part 2 / Jason Ryberg / 48
Sunshine (A Love Letter To Kansas City) /
  Mz Angela Roux / 51

Finding Zen in Cow Town / Shawn Pavey

In Kansas City's Union Station,
monks gathered to shake
colored sand that would become not sand,
but *mandala*.

And here — pay attention now —
here is where it gets interesting:
a boy, three, maybe four,
saunters under the cordons
to do a little soft shoe
while monks ate, one assumes,
a simple meal.

Intricate designs and sharp, colored lines —
some no wider than a single small grain —
became the dust and scuffle of a child's abandon.

When asked, on the news that night,
what he thought of the security footage
of the child's sand dancing, of the mother's
quick grab and fast retreat, a monk replied, smiling,
We swept it up and started over.
We will just have to work faster now.

In a few days, in an unveiling ceremony,
attendees marveled
ooh and *ahh*.

After all of the cameras packed away,
monks swept the second attempt
into a sacred vessel and poured it
into the waters of the Missouri
for good fortune.

The mandala, you see,
is like this poem in which we find ourselves
this very moment.
Dance in it, kick it around under
the soles of your feet.
Sweep it up.
Pour it in a river.

Let it all wash out to sea.

It's a Food Town / Jose Faus

She says it has always been a blues town
even when it was a jazz town
but she's wrong it's a food town
because I can't choose between
costillas en chile verde up on Summit
or *samosas* piping hot on Lexington
scalding pho in the market
dumplings on 39th street
chicken spiedini on fifth
or gyros falafel and pizza at the curb
I don't want to argue Gates Bryants
Jackstack LC's Oklahoma Joe's
or your granddady's all night long
Italian and Austrian in the freight
peppercorns above the trains
peaches from the tree or double cheese
& grilled onions on Broadway or Baltimore
taquitos on Central or Independence Avenues
greens in Eden's garden
strutting chickens north and south
pollos ricos shrimp *biryani* sashimi
remoulade *ooh la la* mix the bunch and bring me
iced sweet tea and bourbon on the side.

Kansas City / Fredric Sims

Kansas City ...
You are fixed in the fibers of my memory.
Always glowing ...
Reflecting everything my heart has
Been collecting over the years.
Like when dad took me to Royals games.
Trust, back then,
Taking the crown
Was a figment of our imagination.
We came,
For the chilli cheese fries to
Know again the smell of hot dogs,
Wooden seats, and in the bliss,
Kiss the summer air.
We left our cares back home
And had a *vaca-for-a-day*
With the boys in blue.
Kansas City ...
Your power and light will always
Have the feel of my first date on its back,
The sensation of that night in December,
Where winter chilled my skin.
Making me long for warmth.
Which I found.
In her gift of words
She showed me parts
Of her self I had not seen.

The things that lay behind
Her blonde hair and blue eyes.
And I longed to see more,
On future days, I hoped,
Were just around the corner of time.
Kansas City ...
I fell in love with jazz inside of you.
It flirted with me from a distance.
The relationship was formed
When horns fit themselves inside of melodies,
Connected to harmonies that lingered,
Like a low cloud full of chords,
Creating for me a new revelation,
Birthing expression out of my soul
In ways I couldn't control.
I had to play.
So much I had to say.
My life story had to be displayed
On this canvas so ...
I made the saxophone my paint brush.
And could not wait to
Compose my first piece.
Kansas City ...
I'll never forget how you captured
The smile of my best friend.
Joy came bursting out of his teeth
As he enjoyed singing Sade.
Sprint Center couldn't contain his voice
The reaction ...

Or better yet
The reflection of him being himself.
A self ...
That is beautiful, and shining
All the more brightly than
I ever thought it would.
I could say more.
There are books worth of stories
Of how you stored me in the night light alone.
Alone.
Yet home.

Muehlebach Hotel, Kansas City / Denise Low

The red-faced clerk leans over the counter
leering at my breasts. My groom stutters.
I grab the single brass key.

Ivy-twilled staircase trim mimics forests.
Globe lighting sheds nightmare tints
muting sofas and walnut wainscoting.

The elevator man speaks minor-key tunes.
His flat eyes are quarter-notes of silence.
The door heaves shut and we ascend.

The final lurch turns our stomachs.
We clamber out of the vertical tunnel
to our room of ginger jar lamps.

We sit speechless. From the window
I scrutinize gray streets until dawn.
Hemingway types tomorrow's paper.

Driving Through Kansas in Late Autumn / Phil Miller

First you see
tar paper, clapboard, old red barn,
yellow trees against a sky
smeared gray.
Then these catch your eye:
tip of weathervane, slow
blade of windmill slicing
air, hawk's slant wing,
curve of crow,
windrow of dishwater hay;
rusty bristleweed, rooster comb
of dry sumac,
a stand of cattle splotched
eggshell, coal, burnt sienna,
before your eyes blur,
let landscape slide
to dusky field and ditch,
to umber, ash, and teal,
to thin streak of rouge,
to one long wash of bruise.

Kansas City Renga / Silvia Kofler

Magnolia tree blooms
sigh beneath spring snow blanket.
Kansas City April

foolishness snickers at city
squirrels digging bulbs, urban

garden booty. Satur-
day evening's Westport pub
patrons mingle at

windblown restaurant patios
listen to local music.

davey's stagecoach / Sharon Eiker

i was grateful for the lack of light
that afternoon.
i wanted to get away
from it all to hide
i was grateful for the scotch
on the rocks too.
let the ice melt until it
tasted just right.
cold cool single malt
becomes scotch and water
then the mind melts down
just right
the worries of the day
become fluid and wash away
with the ebb and flow of
meaningless conversation
and the occasional crack of pool balls
old time rock and roll
on the juke box
she's got a ticket to ride
and she don't care

The Cowboys Got Anchored Here
by Demonic Forces / Ezhno Martin

      That thousand cigarette stare
            is looking mighty fine
on your tight ass
          Mr Bookstore Cowboy
     Marlboro Man
              of the pulp paperback
     leaning against the dollar rack reading
            sometimes seven hours a day
      with a land-line cordless phone
            next to a glass of flavored vodka
     and hoo-ha tincture
             mysteriously always half full
       hanging off the newspaper machine

     You are the underground gay love story
          of the land of Dorthy
              like unkilled meat
and dead end streets
              for suburban communities
     that never came to be

            heart attack of America
                  and every cholesterol cliché that
goes along with it
        you are delicious
           for how we lust after you
           like we can never know any better

Expelled Prophets: A Never City / Crista Siglin

We are announced to the city
and to each other
by our conspicuous stations from which
we stand looking out on the edges.
When I watch my love,
he reaches out, but the street
cats on 39th
are not as friendly
as those on 31st.
Can I no longer call
the arms of my love similar to that
of a tree?
How legitimate
must a child be
to one day negotiate himself
a man worthy
of his own shadow?

How many shades
can a city hold
before one within it
bursts into a terrible
sequence of verses
and dreams that exchange
themselves with the night true
beneath the dark
emerald of Gillham park
without permission
from the dreamer?

It could be the
temperament of each haunt
we made was never what we thought
it was when we came
to be changed into our own
heroes, but
more likely, we confused
the buildings' verb
tenses—unaware that they
had been what they were
for long before
we were what we were.

We never know
what trails us.
We want to be prophets,
but are uncertain whether
prophets have
aspirations, and when we
see Post-it notes
on the pavement lining the
park, we make no motion
to pick them up.
We only ask questions that
we already know the answers to,
and to people that
will give us those answers.

It is safe in our heads and
when we finally get up in the
late morning
to get dressed, but
we have no idea
whether we are pulling
archetypes over our heads.

Jackson County Baby / Jeanette Powers

My city likes to beat itself up
pretend that state line
divides savage from civilized
like we don't I-70 ourselves east to west
like we don't 435 the big circle
like we don't know both do barbeque, races, lakes
pools, parks, mom and pop stores, keep faith
next to big box, and paycheck to paycheck
you know you got family
you don't mention much
that lives in Sugar Creek, JoCo
Lake Lotawana or the Dotte.

Still ya'll horrified if some Coaster catcalls:
        there's no place like home!
and ya hafta-gotta-pride-requires-it, retort:
              I'm from Missouri, man!

We slap down any non-local
and need to immediately educate them
on the fact that our city lives in 2 states
and that we don't have anything
                to do with ourselves.

UNTITLED # 3 / Brandon Whitehead

So I'm sitting out on the sidewalk
in front of Prospero's Books
late at night,
watching the traffic go by,
beeping and honking
with lights flashing like
they're talking while the
people wander in and out
of the bar on the corner:
yuppies and bums,
strippers and poets,
dancing so they don't get too close,
like they're magnets or something,
polarized for their own protection
from each other,
each on a course
that's evasive at best,
doing laundry, getting tattoos,
beer, the daily news with
cigarettes and coffee, eating
and walking, talking and
drinking in little shops.
It's a last supper out here
and each apostle's got
his job to do, leaving scorch marks
on the concrete,
bits of paper with old numbers
under empty cups …
This is primordial stuff,
this Mulligan's stew of us;

give it heat and pressure
and some strange green
lightning bolt and 39th street
might sit up, scratch its ass
and mutter …
and what would it say
about you
or me
while we hang on for our lives
like we do every day,
and still are,
sitting on the sidewalk,
drifting down the street
like we're secret words
written with invisible ink
on ancient tea leaves
that get scattered
by celestial winds
that no one,
no one,
ever
reads.

Kansas City / Xanath Caraza

Bosque art Deco de concreto
con ecos de Charlie Parker y jazz
confluencia de emplumadas serpientes de agua

Caravaggio asado del medio oeste
con un Tom Benton
doblemente quemado y fisgón

Poemas a la luna roja
en osage, francés, inglés
ebonics y español

Oraciones a una ancestral
diosa maya de jade,
a la crisis nuclear de Japón
y la guerra en Libia

La migra quizá me confunda
sin tiempo para guardar
ni poemas ni plumas

Sonidos del pasado y presente,
náhuatl, wolof,
inglés y español
producen espirales
símbolos lingüísticos,
tornados en el alma

Ramas color turquesa,
dragones de buena suerte,
tambores djembé,
el verde del quetzal

Bakalva ámbar y
los poemas de Sor Juana,
reviven los muros
de la ciudad

Kansas City / Xanath Caraza

Art Deco forest of concrete
with echoes of Charlie Parker's jazz
confluence of plumed serpents of water

Grilled Midwest Caravaggio
with a twice baked
peeping Tom Benton on the side

Poems for *la luna roja*
in Osage, French, English,
Ebonics *y español*

Prayers to an ancient
Mayan jade goddess,
for Japan's nuclear crisis
and the Libyan war

La migra perhaps *me confunda*
with no time for collecting
poems nor pens

Sounds from the past and present,
Nahuatl, Wolof,
English *y español*
producing spiral
linguistic symbols,
tornadoes in the soul

Turquoise branches,
good fortune dragons,
Djembe drums,
the green of quetzal

Amber baklava and
Sor Juana's poems,
renewed life to the murals
of the city walls

A Barbequed Life (1967) / Stanley E. Banks
(For My Grandmother)

At Georgia's bootleg-beer house
on 10th and Vine, every holiday
the smell of sizzling beef and
its juices roasting in garlic, onions
and tomato sauce floated through
10th, 11th, and 12th streets.

> Georgia's husband, a World War I
> veteran from 1917 to 1919,
> grilled in the backyard showing the skills
> he learned while serving in France.

As folks woke up on Vine Street,
Georgia already would be boasting
with her bull-horn voice,
> *Y'all can steal my sauce,*
> *but if I run upon you,*
> *I'm gonna be your boss.*

> Jay Bone, Georgia's son, set up
> his four piece horn section early
> so the fellas could eat biscuits, barbeque,
> and practice in between their greasin'.

Six Bits, the barber, would holler back
from his next door porch,

*Georgia, my thick hot-peppered brisket
is what every Vine Street heifer needs
when I fix it.*

    The days of barbequing
    freed the air for the black folks
    of Vine Street who lived
    lives hungry for
    Jim Crow liberation.

For the whole of these days
Georgia and Six Bits would battle
for barbeque bragging rights
playing the dozens on each other's momma
trying to come up
with the coolest insult.

    Georgia always got the last lick,
    *I told you clowns
    once you taste my voodoo
    hickory barbeque
    baby, you'll lose your damn mind
    and beg to call me, divine.*

No Blue Mondays, No Smoky Horns / Steven H. Bridgens

I mourn the loss of those dark, sad clubs
and the blue horns and shiny ebony pianos
that played this river town.

I mourn the passing of those nightspots,
the Playmore, Lucille's Paradise, Tootie's
Mayfair, the Antler's Club and the Century
Club now all gone to un-mowed vacant lots,
to fading silent memories played out on
scratchy black circles of sound.

I mourn the passing of that lost town,
that once gleaming city on the bluffs
that really lived where now wander
lonely those tuneless streets and ride
the ghostly street cars we've paid for twice.

I mourn the death of those clubs, that music,
and the real Kings and Queens of KC Soul
now buried deep beneath the HIP-HOPocracy
of the thinly veiled racist facades wholly-owned
subsidiaries of the you-know-who's–all served up to us
by the phony political hacks that want it all — *Family Style!*

Yes, I mourn the inevitable ascendancy of the do-gooder,
the bluenose, the prude, the developer and his pal,
the big banker and finally, the glad hand greeter at
the bronze door all knowing so well what's good for
Our Town ... and their bankroll!

Attention: Oak Street Residents / Gustavo Adolfo Aybar

At our new apartment, rented to create space
for the baby — a bulletin board sign reads,

*... African American male, six feet tall,
mid-twenties, with cornrows ... call the police.*

Positioned two inches closer to constellations,
of equal complexion and age range,

I wear the gray hoodie required
of every Jumpstart volunteer.

He has been seen in a black-hooded
sweatshirt or a gray puffy jacket.

Erika thinks it funny. It remains our joke for days,
— when will I turn myself in.

I think ... I was at the library, my Don Quijote class
or tutoring. I hope the cornrows Karen will style for me today

will be different. I worry, while crumpling the paper,
if our baby will also bear the burden of my dark skin.

untitled k.c. poem / Jacob Johanson

where you come from matters adds
its cadence to dreams illuminates
the bookstores of your personal heavens
defines angels and visionaries
engine sound of cars passing
through concrete and bone to hum
against your teeth
while deer invade the suburbs
the cawing of crows hot-wired to nerves
to joyride myth
left abandoned along I-70
praying for a cheap tow —

my angels
spend their days polishing haloes
on 39th in kansas city
all of us working
at the minimum wage dream factory
turning out verbs for pennies
and the right to claim a street-corner
at the intersection of unsubmitted poems
and improbable movie scenes

the long drawn philosophies of monday sunsets
ghosts snicker at the opening of beer bottles
sidewalks fearless in the knowledge of our pacing
and somewhere a trumpet or a viola or a saxophone

winding down to hang a note on
the closed eye image of kansas dusk
horizons that whisper of far cities
goldrush and homestead hanging
along the dimming light as we
casually
put the orchestra
at full throttle

Broadway Street / Victor Clevenger

Buttercup yellow boots with this
toad-belly-tinted dress
is the perfect mix of hideous
& she doesn't give a damn
what she looks like at one
o'clock in the morning, or one
o'clock in the afternoon.

she walks beside me & I
don't give a damn what she
looks like either.

*Should we stick-up the corner
store & rob 'em blind, baby?*
she asks & I remind her that
she is the only silly twat
wearing buttercup yellow
boots.

She laughs & calls me a pussy
in black plastic glasses; I roll
my eyes & open the door.

The corner store smells like
corndogs, & she hates that smell,
oh well.

I can eat a half dozen with
ketchup, but no mustard & I
ask her,

*Baby, do you remember when the
Blockbuster Video store used to sit
next to Chubby's Diner?*

The Benefits of Age / John Dorsey

damian & rebecca witness a shooting
in the parking lot of their motel

which may or may not
double as the bathroom of town topic

as i watch a shooting star
shimmy through the night sky
like grease lightning
sailing past my window

waiting until morning
for bacon & fried eggs

ignoring the raisin bran & fresh fruit
as if i were dodging a bullet.

Saturday Night At Longview Lake, Disguised As Purgatory Cove / John Mark Eberhart

Henry's dead now, of course, and that boy must be a
middle aged man. Hepburn too, is gone, and the movie
itself seems a relic from another age, when movies really
were golden. I do not know why I came up here.
I do not know why I rented this damned boat, only to sit here
in dark water on a clammy September night.
I am bullshitting myself. Of course I know why.
I know because I always know, these days. I came up here
because I was missing you. You played Ethel Thayer, once,
in the stage version they did at that little college in Missouri.
You were too young for the role, sure, but they padded you
a little and dressed you in plain clothes to hide your curves,
and everyone said your voice was the equal of Hepburn's
herself, just not quite so shaky. I have always wanted to see
the place for myself, where they rolled the cameras,
where Henry and that boy had to wear wetsuits under their
costumes because it was such a cold shoot. Yes my love,
just like life can sometimes be, so fracturing in terms of cold,
to take your life from you while you were still so young,
beautiful, and we had so much left to do. I came up here
to drink bourbon and sit in this rented bass boat, and try to
remember how you were before you got sick. I recall another
play you were in at one time: was it a Beckett piece?
Anyway, you spent your entire time onstage in a trashcan,
and I was sitting in the audience laughing at you so hard.

Your performance was so convincing that after just ten
minutes of dialogue, I forgot that I was married to you.
And when you met me backstage after, still in that absurd
getup, I kissed you and told you I'd loved every moment.
Tonight, here in this real south Kansas City lake,
playing the role of Purgatory Cove from a fiction called
On Golden Pond, I wish I could tell you the same thing
about the non-fiction life we once lived together.
It was the role of a lifetime, and I loved every moment
on stage, with you.

Summer Magic / Joseph Davis

All along the circumference of this swirling curl of lonesome;
the evening's humidity colludes with fireflies alighting on my
aching aliveness. I swat idly at a wandering moth of some
kind with my right hand. My left hand is clenched, fist-tight,
as if holding a Cracker Jack prize, but I am holding nothing
but ennui and desire. Denny Matthews narrates another
Royals abysmal loss, while I contemplate the word *evening*:
that is, a balancing, a leveling. Slowly, a nascent indigo shifts
the equilibrium of twilight into night, its patient silence
broken by the giddy laughter of a skateboarding kid speeding
under the brightening beams of the streetlight across the
street and just to the left of our front porch, which is dark.
A night that yearns for hammock laziness, and I am sitting,
pensively, like coils on a discarded bed frame.

But then, I sense the silent swing of our screen door opening
as Lulu sneaks out in bare feet. I turn too late to prevent
the ice cube sliding down the back of my tank top.
Her giggles thwart the silence of my solitude.
Wet, and welcome in its dripping cold surprise,
I unclench my fist to swat away her other hands,
formed in the puckish claw of trying to tickle me.
I stand up from our front porch steps, pulling her to me
with a desperation I no longer conceal when I am around her.
Silently, I dare to laugh that laugh again, so I can halt it
in her throat with the kind of kiss that Summer double-dog
dares lovers give one another. Heatwaves give way and rise
to the stars adding luster to night's canopy of sky: deepening,
reveling, welcoming.

Whatcha thinkin' 'bout? Lulu asks, clasping her hands
underneath my tank top, not minding the perspiration
on me while I sit brooding. We begin this subtle sway,
invisible to anyone who'd see us. I say nothing for almost
a minute, content to rest my chin on her head, before I say,

*Not a damn thing, babe. Just lettin' summer work its magic.
Just lettin' the summer work its magic.*

Deep Chigger Shade / W. E. Leathem

The fist of god smashes
down on the *'nine,*
grinds out the butt-end of its anger,

sends everyone scattering,
searching the bottom of pockets,
the saucer on the chest of drawers,
the dashboard ashtray.

Those who can
scrounge the price of admission
and are off to a flick.

Those with enough
for a cup, hold up
in the coffee shop,
back in back, out of the way,
re-reading the same page of paper
day after day

never seeming to tire
of yesterday's news,
stretching that single coffee
across afternoons.

The lucky slip away,
strays vanishing for days
on end behind air conditioned doors

sipping the fabled beakers
of cheap beer
that sweat circular scars
on favorite end tables,
toes chilling on carpets
in the pale rerun glow.

Maybe later,
after the sun goes down,
they'll go for a drive,
check on the old lady
who sits on her porch
lights off,
a bowl of water and a rag
in her lap,
mouthing prayers of thanks
for the mercy
of oscillating fans.

And all the economic sinners —
worse than horse thieves —
were last seen on Monday
going over the side
into the deep chigger shade,

or up beneath the overpass
where hell's chariots
churn the unforgiving asphalt breeze.

Surrogate City / Huascar Medina

Mama, *Estoy Bien.*

Mother KC has adopted me.
She too wears ironed garments
of concrete and glass,
winks at me to cross the streets,
reminds me I am cared for
through sirens in the air.

She hums a highway lullaby
of old Paseo *Puente;*
so I may pass the nights,
skylines don't resemble
mi vieja san ciudad in peace.

She embraces
your son
the sun
el sol
my soul.

KC has been good to me.

Kansas City: After Filming, Robert Altman's
Musicians Stop by the Club / Kevin Rabas

The New Yorkers blow into town
   and blow fast on sax on the stand.
Our drummers can't keep up.
Then a kid, 15, from Paseo
   sits in—all lightning and fire,
limbs like willows in wind,
   he stays, plays,
a cig tip in an onyx night,
hands and legs a blur.

Old Bill rubs his wrists, buys me a drink,
   says, *That kid. He does us good.*
                     This city. His hands.

Revival / Glenn North

There is a place where parched lips
kiss warped reeds and cramped fingers
stroke strings and keys
filling the air with melodies.
And resurrected rhapsodies
capture the cadence of ancient chants
where shackles are removed
and our ancestors dance
in anticipation of liberty
and every note that's played
is dedicated to their memory.

There is a place where each heartache
and every sharp pain
can be smoothed and soothed
by a medicinal refrain
the story of King David makes it plain:

And it came to pass,
when the evil spirit from God
was upon Saul that David took a harp,
and played with his hand:
so Saul was refreshed, and was well,
and the evil spirit departed from him.

You see this divinely inspired requiem
came forth from a glorious past
and though it defies description

we choose to call it Jazz
and ever since this music
emerged from space and time
it has found a permanent residence
on 9 + 9 and Vine.
Someday soon you'll travel there
to escape from emails,
cell phones and faxes,
from being overworked and underpaid
and paying too many taxes.
This is the place where even Struggle
kicks off his shoes and relaxes
and the only war that will ever take place
is the *battle of the saxes.*

This is the place where Jazz
is served up as a sensual delight...
and it smells like grandmother's chitlins
'cause she always cooks 'em just right,
and it tastes like the peach cobbler
she makes that gets better with every bite,
and it feels like love's very first kiss
shared in the soft moonlight,
and it looks like Susanna Jones
when she wears that red dress,
Lord, what a beautiful sight,
and it sounds like the Jazz Disciples
smooth on a blue Monday night
or like Gabriel's trump at the Rapture
just before we take flight.

So these ministers of music
are awaiting your arrival
wanting to provide you
with orchestral comfort
as you witness the Revival
because jazz, like matter,
can't be destroyed
it only changes forms
and the historic intersection
of 18th and Vine
is where jazz will be reborn.

Then we will cherish
this noble noise
and glow in the cool of its heat
as the caramel coated cacophony
creates a sonically hypnotic beat
that can only ever be heard
through the tapping soles of the feet
and as willing slaves to the rhythm
our freedom will be complete.

Kansas City Nights / William Peck

There's just something that draws me
into the shadow-shift evening
'neath hunching street lights,
in the din of some crowd
on a Kansas City night.

You got the clack of the pool balls,
the laughter of sluts,
the bombast of the drunk
with a ten gallon gut
buried 'neath the burnished brass of the bar,
and there's Cliff with his cue stick
and a big fat cigar,

and there's the girl that I know
with a radio voice
who's twisted up inside
like a blue bag of pretzels,
but she's got the joke
and the winning smile
that usually protects her,

and I know how it feels
to be that someone
who's always faking laughter,
always has the answers,
has it altogether.

That's why I'm here
drinking dark beer
and talking to these strangers.
You got rock n roll,
blues and soul,
pretty girls with perfect curls,
painted lips and plastic kisses
to keep your mind from burning time
in the alleyway
where the bullies hang
with no other mission
than to kick your ass
and keep right on kickin'.

So I keep dropping bills
on top of the bar.
Look at me, baby.
I've come so far.
I'm smoking like a chimney
on a three-dog night.
I got my ale and my whiskey,
and I'm feeling alright.
Until last call comes
and I have to go home
and face the mirror
when I'm all alone
but for the austere walls
and their paint all chipping,
a bed and a blanket
and a fucked-up ceiling
and a flip-flop night

as I'm waiting for tomorrow
so I can hit the street
and find a beat
to distract me from my sorrow.

Until evening comes
and cabs start prowling.
When the drinks are poured
and I find accord
with my stomach growling
over a Styrofoam bowl
of hot creole;
when everybody's smiling
with a drink in their hands
and a swing in their hips
to the cadence of a band.

And I'll run into Cliff and I'll shoot some stick,
or find the radio girl and talk some shit,
and it'll all go down on a Kansas City night,
on a shadow-shift evening,
'neath hunching street lights.

james street 3 a.m. (or, view from the roof of a '57 ford) / Victor Smith

greedy's got one crazy eye
shows the future if you stare too long
says i'm gonna shoot that radio
if it plays one more sad song
the moon is overflowing with jack rabbits mad dogs
and hookers with bad feet and the whole damn thing
is pouring down on 3 a.m. james street
the air is heavy with the musky smell
you only get when the money is gone
and the narcs are trading snitch cards
in the back alley for a song
well tony's stayed out too long again
now the half-way house on truman
won't let him back in
sometimes it feels like james street
is the only mama tony's got
now he's looking to trade what god gave him
for a hot meal and a cot
young bloods with cartoon names
spit out nightmares in little plastic sacks
they know that love has never been the cure
it's all about the comeback
sunshine's running for the liquor store
with someone else's bad check
trailing blue clouds of cordite
and cheap menthol cigarettes
the wind whistles through a chain link fence
like a twisted love gone wrong
and greedy says i'm gonna shoot that radio
if it plays one more fuckin' sad song

The War Goes Ever On From The City Where It Began / Jason Preu

Outside my newly-washed office windows
    breathes Kansas City,
neatly scarred by highways —

reminders of a war the city once fought —
    still fights —
between a desire
      to be together
    and a desire
to be apart.

The city breathes.

The city grows —
    like every other city in this country —
Kansas City knows
      no borders;
      crosses state lines in name and occupation,
      eats neighboring towns for breakfast,
      obliterates puny customs in its way …

and this city will,
    one day,
ooze into other cities —

St. Louis
Omaha
Des Moines —
and they will all breathe
as one

having been brought together
   by the shared scars
of common and quiet
   ambivalent wars.

What's Up, Kansas City? / Serenity

34 and counting that's what the news story said.
We continue to serve a mixed plate of murder and mayhem
but this is not something that will be served at Gates with a
platter of ribs or tasted at Danny's while the blues trumpet
plays instead of blue the fountains flow with blood.
The next homicide will be shown live at 5.

So what's up, Kansas City?

The heart of the nation but our main arteries are blocked;
with each death we are diminishing our future.
Your sons', daughters', and grandchildrens' smiles are broken
and refuted, families placed in fear of the knock at the door
as the sirens are near the sound of mothers' cries cascade
the media groups and airwaves.

What's up, Kansas City? Can you hear me?

I have plenty to say from the dilapidated building on Prospect
to the crack houses on Askew west of the Country Club Plaza
to Ward Parkway; our streets are warzones and the Attorney
General has stepped away. The chief of staff and leaders have
all gone on *lunch break*. We are DYING for you to save us.
With each day we want to know what's up
and why can't our city be safe?

So if you are listening Kansas City, please tell me. What's up?

Scenes From 39th St. Part 2 / Jason Ryberg

what's all this living for, anyway?
-ancient Sufi proverb

Well, here we are again,
drinking beer on the far, bright shore
of 39th and Bell (a.k.a. the palatial front porch
of Prospero's Bookstore) when, suddenly,
the rooster ring-tone of my cell-phone
goes off and it's mom calling
(all the way from Salina, KS) to tell me
there's a big, ugly storm marauding
our way (as if we couldn't see the signs, ourselves,
but I say, *thanks anyway, Ma.*
Tell Dad he still owes me a twenty for that
Royals / Red Sox game last week. Have a good night.)

But it does get me to pondering out-loud
if this year or maybe the next could be
the year that the Hillbilly X-tian Rapture,
the second American Civil War and / or
that giant meteor people have been talking about
for years now (like a frustrated lover just about
to go crazy or give it up) finally comes.

I suppose, in the meantime,
we (meaning (this time) Johanson and Cunnyngham,
Whitehead, Leathem and me) should just keep on
keepin' on with our usual any-given-night-of-
the-week routine: talking politics, movies and books,
telling tall tales of wildly glorious misfortunes and tragi-
comic misadventures from the sunny slopes of long ago,

gawking at girls (of often dangerously
indeterminate ages) as they parade and runway by,
even occasionally wagering on
the erratic behavior of cockroaches
to see who buys the next twelve pack.

Damn. How many years have we been at this?
How many years has some more or less
unwaveringly consistent variation
of this particular street corner court
been holding forth?

How is it a year ago feels like a decade
while some half-remembered something or other
that went down ten years back
somehow seems like... yesterday?

And here we are, the five of us,
adrift and bobbing along in that nebulous neutral zone
between *not as dumb as I used to be* and
some girl saying, *you're just a little too old for me*,
between the Bloomsbury Group and The Lost Boys,
between the Isle of Davos and The Island Of Misfit Toys.

And, like the overgrown Peter Parker / college kid /
as-of-yet-still-undiscovered artistes we may very well be,
we'll probably keep on keepin' the faith for as long
as we're breathing (without tanks, at least).

And besides, what the hell else are we gonna do
with our time?

And, like that much misunderstood, much maligned
Frankenstein Monster of our age, Roy Batty,
we will probably be left desperately wanting *more life, fuckers(!)*
when our custom designed carriages and rickshaws arrive
to carry us off, respectively, to the Big Who Knows Where?

Meanwhile, back down here
at the big pay-per-view / pay-to-play main event
of Just Another Friday Night In Kansas City, MO,
the crew has somehow spontaneously multiplied
into a crowd and there seems to be a heated debate
going down about who would win in a fight
between Magneto and Doctor Doom.

And someone's pulled out the ever-reliable
Kennedy Trail of The Dead (and maybe even
a little something about the admittedly inherent mysteries
of Building 7) while someone else is taking bets on
which self-righteous, holy-rollin' culture warrior /
rodeo clown the Republicans are gonna be bat-shit
crazy enough to even think about nominating.

And the sky suddenly goes all
charcoal / horror movie back-drop.

And the thunder comes out like someone's
Strict Father Model of a God took a drunken tumble
down a long flight of stairs.

And the first drop of rain
hits the sidewalk with a sizzling

POP!

Sunshine (A Love Letter To Kansas City) / Mz Angela Roux

I love …
love to rise early on Saturn's morning, feel his rings
feel his rings like hula hoops around my childlike heart
skip! jump in my car, roll down 71
sit giddy geeked in front of Scooters
peering down a pristine 47th Street
into the darkness of Cleaver Blvd
to see her awaken from her slumber
proud sons and daughters skitter about her streets
like well-dressed honeybees
feverishly walking, talking, shopping
from one flower to the next
some call it people watching
but I'm a student!
I'm a student of interaction
so call me a major in humanities
she is alive and radiant
and I am turned on
reminiscent of the right combination of man and cologne
aromatic ecstasy seems to be turning into a lost art form
like fathers, chivalry, and 50th wedding anniversaries

too many of us going half on babies
too many of us going 50 percent
50 percent of us don't have whole-hearted
perseverance to love

we can't reconcile our differences
so we lament over paradise lost while we sip coffee
we all be searching for sunny days
we all be searching for a sunny daze
bring me sunshine!
sushine! smolder over so vines grow wild over 18th Street
sunshine! reflect rays turning broken hearts of glass
into rainbows at 39th
sunshine!
gleam!
sparkle!

KC you are my sunshine!
KC you are my lover!
KC you are my friend!
KC you are burnt ends slathered with Gates!

Hiiiiii May I Help Yooooooouuuu!!

KC you are gizzards packed in red and white boxes!
Go Chicken Goooooo!!!
KC you are a maverick Texan turned Chief!
KC you are a Kangaroo suspended in rare air
on brick buildings
KC you are Satchel, Buck, Jackie
KC you are a city of Kings not *Killaz*
KC you are Royal
KC you are Cobras marching down Grand Blvd
KC you are a lyrical legend born on 57th and Highland
KC you are the Bloodstone giving way to LoKey

KC you are Oleta, Ida, Hagenbach and Monae
KC you are trendy like Kate Spade
KC you are blue cool fountains springing
KC you are my native tongue
KC you are beautiful!
KC you are beautiful!
KC you are beautiful!

KC you are home!

Gustavo Adolfo Aybar is a Dominican writer, raised in New York, Los Angeles, and Miami Beach. He graduated from the University of Missouri-Kansas City where he received his MA in Romance Languages & Literature. His chapbook, *Between Line Breaks* was released in 2016 through Spartan Press. His first collection, *We Seek Asylum*, will be released early 2017 through Willow Books. Currently Aybar is working on a new poetry collection and on translating the works of Mexican author/playwright Glafira Rocha from Spanish to English. Some translations of Rocha's stories can be found in the online journals *EZRA, Asymptote Journal* and The Brooklyn Rail's *InTranslation Journal*.

Stanley E. Banks. He is an Assistant Professor and Artist-In-Residence at Avila University since 1997. Banks had his 5th book of poetry, *Blue Issues,* published in 2013 by Naomi Bards Press in Kansas City, Missouri. His other 4 books are *Blue Beat Syncopation* (2003), *On 10Th Alley Way* (1981), *Coming From A Funky Time And Place* (1988), and *Rhythm And Guts* (1992). While attending Howard University in Washington, D.C. as a Graduate student in the Fall of 1980, he met Sterling Brown, the great Harlem Renaissance Poet, and in the following year, he received the Langston Hughes Prize For Poetry in 1981. He has won Honorary Awards which includes a Proclamation For Achievement in 2002 from the Mayor of Kansas City, Missouri. For the entire year of 2002, his life and history in publishing was exhibited at The Black Archives of Mid-America, Inc. Further, in 1989 he was awarded the National Endowment For The Arts Fellowship/Grant for his poetry. He has been published in many Literary Magazines/Journals around the country.

Steven H. Bridgens: Born: Kansas City, Missouri, Planet Earth, 1949, the year of the first Soviet nuclear test. Parents: healers, one trod the dark path and one the light. Siblings: one of each, both younger, iconoclasts and artists. Progeny: one son, a man now with his own trajectory and dreams Current Fascinations: words, painting, sculpture, the ancient world or the idea of it, particularly the rebuilding of it, silence and the absence of it, sleep and the same, dead bluesmen, ancient Asian poets, the demi-monde, espionage, imagined, not real, the primeval forest of Buddhism in all its humble glory, the savage comic tyranny of the political stage, the toxic and liberating proscenium of the internet, the dark Jungian depths of the self, the flickering colored shadows of the cinema and architecture, the utopian possibilities of life on garden earth with our liberated sentient friends. Death: certain as to its eventuality but uncertain as to its time. Indifferent, but not unconcerned.

Xánath Caraza es viajera, educadora, poeta y narradora. Es columnista de *La Bloga, Smithsonian Latino Center, Periódico de Poesía, Revista Literaria Monolito y Revista Zona de Ocio.* Sus poemarios son *Lágrima roja* (2017), *Sin preámbulos / Without Preamble* (2017), *Le sillabe del vento / Sílabas de viento* (2017), *Donde la luz es violeta / Where the Light is Violet* (2016), *Tinta negra / Black Ink* (2016), *Ocelocíhuatl* (2015), *Sílabas de viento / Syllables of Wind* (2014), *Noche de colibríes* (2014), *Corazón pintado* (2012, 2015), *Conjuro* (2012), su libro de relatos, *Lo que trae la marea / What the Tide Brings* (2013) y su segunda colección de relatos, *Pulsación*, está en progreso.

Xánath Caraza is a traveler, educator, poet and short story writer. She is a columnist of *La Bloga, Smithsonian Latino Center, Periódico de Poesía* and *Revista Zona de Ocio*. Her books are *Lágrima roja* (2017), *Sin preámbulos / Without Preamble* (2017), *Le sillabe del vento / Sílabas de viento* (2017), *Donde la luz es violeta / Where the Light is Violet* (2016), *Tinta negra / Black Ink* (2016), *Ocelocíhuatl* (2015), *Sílabas de viento / Syllables of Wind* (2014), *Noche de colibríes* (2014), *Corazón pintado* (2012, 2015), *Conjuro* (2012), her short story collection, *Lo que trae la marea / What the Tide Brings* (2013) and her second short story collection, *Pulsación,* is in progress.

Victor Clevenger hopes for the more exciting side of death, as he spends his days in a Madhouse and his nights writing poetry. He sleeps with his second ex-wife and raises his six children in a small town northeast of Kansas City, MO. Selected pieces of his work have appeared at, *Poems-For-All, Chiron Review, GTK Journal, Yellow Chair Review, Rat's Ass Review, Blink Ink, Thirteen Myna Birds,* the *2016 Hessler Street Fair Poetry Anthology* (Crisis Chronicles Press), *Delirious: A Poetic Celebration of Prince* (NightBallet Press, 2016), *Prompts!* (39 West Press, 2016). Victor's poetry collections include *Come Here* (Least Bittern Books, 2016), *The More Exciting Side Of Death* (Epic Rites Press/Tree Killer Ink, 2016), and *Soulwhore* (Svensk Apache, 2017).

Joseph Davis has been a lifelong resident of Kansas City and started writing poetry around age 14. He graduated (and survived) catholic indoctrination at Bishop Hogan, graduating 1979 and Benedictine College with a BA in English in 1992. When not writing songs, poems and composing music, his true loves are playing electric bass and keyboards and enjoying just how inept he is at both. These days he's a baker at Doughnut Lounge and digging it.

John Dorsey lived for many years in Toledo, Ohio. He is the author of several collections of poetry, including *Teaching the Dead to Sing: The Outlaw's Prayer* (Rose of Sharon Press, 2006), *Sodomy is a City in New Jersey* (American Mettle Books, 2010), *Appalachian Frankenstein* (GTK Press, 2015) and *Being the Fire* (Tangerine Press, 2016). He is the current Poet Laureate of Belle, MO. He may be reached at archerevans@yahoo.com.

John Mark Eberhart (1960 – 2013) was born in St. Joseph, Missouri, less than a mile from the house in which Jesse James was assassinated by Robert Ford, but grew up mostly in the St. Louis and Kansas City metropolitan areas. He earned a bachelor's degree in journalism and economics from the University of Missouri-Columbia in 1983, and later earned a master of arts in English at the University of Missouri-Kansas City in 1998. From 1983 to 1986 he was the environmental reporter for the Baton Rouge State-Times, and in 1987 became a staff writer at The Kansas City Star, where he worked until 2009, serving as the newspaper's highly acclaimed book review editor for ten of those years. In January 2010 he joined the Johnson County (Kansas) Library as an information specialist and in November 2010 was promoted to serve as the library's Readers Advisory Coordinator, a position he held until his death in 2013. He is the author of two books of poetry, *Night Watch* (2005) and *Broken Time* (2008), published by Mid-America Press. A posthumous third collection of poetry is forthcoming.

Sharon Eiker was born in rural Missouri. She is a poet, song writer, and visual Artist. Sharon has hosted the Writer's Place open mic for twenty five years and was a founding member of that project serving on their board for over twenty years. Sharon's work can be found in many anthologies and chapbooks. Most recently *The Second Coming is a Woman* was published by Spartan Press. Sharon has never sought fame and fortune and they have graciously passed her by. Sharon recently founded Jump Start Art a 501(C)3 non profit foundation whose mission is to connect emerging Artists with community resources. Sharon's definition of poetry is, *The song of the soul sung to the beat of the heart.* Her motto is, *create a world you can stand to live in.*

José Faus is a native of Bogota, Colombia and a long time resident of the Kansas City area. He is a graduate of the University of Missouri at Kansas City where he received degrees in English/Creative Writing & Journalism and Painting/Studio Art. He is a founder of the Latino Writers Collective and is currently president of the board of the Writers Place. He also sits on the boards of UMKC Friends of the Library and Charlotte Street Foundation.

Jacob Johanson has made his way up a heavy hill of silence and stands now wondering at the rhythm of breath, seeking word. He is an unrepentant dreamer who lives in Kansas City, KS with his wife, the poet Abigail Beaudelle.

Silvia Kofler, born in Austria, lives in Kansas City, Missouri. She portrayed the German wife and mother in the independent film *The Dome of Heaven* by Diane Glancy. She is a poet, translator, educator, actor and bon vivant whose writings have been published in many journals and anthologies like *The Book of Hopes and Dreams to benefit Spirit Aid in the UK, The Sixth Surface: Steven Holl Lights the Nelson-Atkins Museum,* and *travelin' music: A Poetic Tribute to Woody Guthrie*. *Radioactive Musings*, a poetry collection, appeared in 2008. *Markers*, a play, won the Plays-In-Progress contest at Rockhurst University. She has read at New York's Poet's House, the Sacramento Poetry Center and at Schokoladen, in Berlin.

W.E. Leathem is founder and co-owner of Prosperos Books and Spartan press and has released 3 volumes of poetry. He lives in Volker with his partner, Leslie, his son and two step daughters.

Denise Low, 2007-9 Kansas Poet Laureate, is award-winning author of *A Casino Bestiary* (Spartan Press 2017); a memoir *The Turtle's Beating Heart*, the University of Nebraska Press's *American Indian Lives Series; Jackalope*, fiction (Red Mountain 2016), *Mélange Block*, poetry (Red Mountain 2014); and others. Low is a past board president of AWP. She blogs, reviews, and co-publishes Mammoth Publications, which specializes in Native books. She teaches in the Baker University School of Graduate and Professional Studies in addition to professional workshops across the country. She taught at Haskell Indian Nations University, where she founded the creative writing program

Ezhno Martin is a Kansas City Queer hearing the call of multiple former eastward homelands. Ezhno doesn't believe in pronouns and doesn't use them, but does believe in making books and tangible pieces of art to take home and love. Ezhno's Press EMP focuses on publishing freaks and females, but will publish dudes down with duende. Ezhno recently broke out of rehab because Ezhno couldn't stand sobriety and the preponderance of positive outlooks concurrently. Ezhno used to have a cat named Furlinghetti, but the cat found Ezhno tedious and stopped showing up for dinner.

Huascar Edil Medina has lived artfully in Topeka, Kansas since 2001 as a writer/actor/singer/artist. His hometown is originally San Antonio, Tx but he does not miss things that do not fit in his ticket pocket. He is the father of a five year old demigod Sebastian Rook Medina. Currently he is a member of Topeka's Speak Easy Poetry Group and the Red Tail Collective in Lawrence. His first published poem appeared in *HomeWords: A Project of the Kansas Poet Laureate*. His words can be found in *Reverberated Echoes: A Kansas City Reader* (Asinimali Publications), *Prompts! : A spontaneous anthology by the poets of Poetic Underground* (39 West Press), and *How to Hang the Moon* (Spartan Press). He is also a magnificent crow.

Philip Miller graduated from Wyandotte High School, Kansas City, KS, in 1961, then received a BA and MA from Emporia St. University 1961-1966 (then Emporia St. Teachers College). While there he studied with Keith Denniston and was editor of Quivira. Miller worked at Kansas City KS Community College from 1976 until 2002. While at KCKCC, he coordinated the college's Basic English program for over 20 years, served as professor of English, taught creative writing, composition, and American literature (in the PACE program). He was president of the Kansas Writers Association, 1987, and hosted their statewide conference. In 1992, Miller was a founding member, then board member and an advisory member of The Writers Place, KCMO. He directed the Riverfront Reading Series from 1987 to 2004. He was considered by many to be the godfather of Kansas City poetry. He passed away in 2011.

Glenn North is the author of *City of Song*, a collection of poems inspired by Kansas City's rich jazz tradition and the triumphs and tragedies of the African American experience. He is a Cave Canem fellow, a Callaloo creative writing fellow and a recipient of the Charlotte Street Generative Performing Artist Award and the Crystal Field Poetry Award. His work has appeared in *Kansas City Voices, One Shot Deal, The Sixth Surface, Caper Literary Journal, Platte Valley Review, Kansas City Voices, KC Studio, Cave Canem Anthology XII, The African American Review*, and *American Studies Journal*. He collaborated with legendary jazz musician, Bobby Watson, on the critically acclaimed recording project, *Check Cashing Day* and was recently appointed Poet Laureate of the 18th & Vine Historic Jazz District.

Shawn Pavey has delivered newspapers, mowed lawns, bagged groceries, cut meat, laid sewer pipe, bussed and waited tables, washed dishes, roofed houses, crunched numbers, rented cars, worked in hotels, worn an apron at Kinko's, and been paid to write everything from résumés to music reviews. Currently, he earns a living as a Technical Recruiter in Mission, KS where he lives with his fiancée and two worthless but adorable cats. He is the author of *Talking to Shadows* (2008, Main Street Rag Press) and *Nobody Steals the Towels From a Motel 6* (2015, Spartan Press), Co-founder and former Associate Editor of *The Main Street Rag Literary Journal*, and a former board member and officer of The Writers Place, a Kansas City-based literary non-profit. His poems, essays, and journalism appear in a variety of national and regional publications. He's hosted poetry readings in bars, coffee shops, haunted houses, bookstores, libraries, front porches, seedy motel rooms, and abandoned warehouses. A graduate of the University of North Carolina's Undergraduate Honors Creative Writing Program, he likes his Tom Waits loud, his bourbon single barrel, and his basketball Carolina Blue.

William Peck has been presenting his poetry to audiences in Kansas City for the last 25 years. He characterizes his own work as being written for the stage and not for the page. He has lived in Kansas City his entire life. He believes that it is the job of the poet to engage the audience, and not that of the audience to apprehend the poet's abstruse insights.

Jeanette Powers is a poet-philosopher-performance artist living in Kansas City, Missouri. She currently works for 39 West Press and directs the generative performing arts venue, Uptown Arts Bar, as well as the arts-based non-profit, Chameleon. Two of her books of poetry were released in 2016, *Tiny Chasm* and *Novel Cliche: aphorisms*. She can most often be found soaking up sunshine with her dog, Ollie-mas, on any nearby river or creek.

Kevin Rabas leads the poetry track at Emporia State University. He has seven books, including *Lisa's Flying Electric Piano*, a Kansas Notable Book and Nelson Poetry Book Award winner, *Eliot's Violin, Sonny Kenner's Red Guitar,* and *Songs for My Father.*

Mz Angela Roux was born and raised in South Kansas City, MO, and has always been a fan of language. Beginning with writing short stories at age eight, she did not find her poetic voice until her early 20s. She describes her poetry as *edutainment* combining witty perspectives on modern day womanhood with social commentary. She participated in *RAW: Spectrum - An Artist Showcase* in April 2014. She was named *Best Spoken Word Act* in Pitch Magazine's *Best of KC 2013* edition. She is the creator and producer of *Estrogen Rush!*, an all-female poetry show, which debuted in November 2012 and had its 2nd show, *Estrogen Rush! A Tribute to Maya Angelou* ran in July 2014. She has featured at the 2010 and 2013 KC Fringe Festival and performed as some of KC's premiere poetry venues.

Jason Ryberg is the author of eleven books of poetry, six screenplays, a few short stories, a box full of folders, notebooks and scraps of paper that could one day be (loosely) construed as a novel, and, a couple of angry letters to various magazine and newspaper editors. He is currently an artist-in-residence at The Prospero Institute of Disquieted P/o/e/t/i/c/s, an editor and designer at Spartan Books and an aspiring b-movie actor. His latest collections of poems are *Head Full of Boogeymen / Belly Full of Snakes* (Spartan Press, 2016) and *Nothing Funny About A Clown After Midnight* (39 West Press, 2017).
He lives in Kansas City, Missouri with a rooster named Little Red and a billygoat named Giuseppe

Serenity has preformed with such groups as Bold New Poets, opened for national poet Sheri *Purpose* Hall in her Fringe Festival production of *MoDézir: The Word Jones Experience* in 2012, been on 90.1fm several times, made multiple appearances on 1590am: The gospel of poets, and has had several poetry features. Serenity is also an accomplished slam poet winning Jazz Poetry Jams in May 2014 and winning 2nd place in the March slamulit qualifier. She is also a founding member of slamulit and helped send the squad to their first national competition. In October 2014 she started a project with Cascade Media group in which she interviewed local poets via the website www.whatsupkansascity.net. At the time the site had virtually no poetry on the site. Serenity worked diligently and built the poetry section in less than a year. She eventually moved into the position of Head of Arts & Entertainment for Cascade Media Group in late 2015.

Crista Siglin is a bundle of somethings seeking more somethings to weave into the mess. She tangles real life phantasmagoria with the unfixed and secret life of objects in her compositions. Membranes are the platform for osmosis, the moment of paradox in which one absolute meets another. This fleeting, sacred moment is a wrenching tenderness. Very interested in combining many aspects of art, she is known for her installations, two and three dimensional works and poetry readings. She grew up in Iowa and uses this fact only when it suits her. Crista is a 2015 recipient of a BFA in Painting and Creative Writing at the Kansas City Art Institute with works appearing at the Kansas City Museum, in Sprung Formal literary magazine, and KCAI's Compendium. She can hardly walk through a garden without befriending a slug; she obnoxiously and persistently holds duets with her orange cat, Apollo, and a French horn

Fredric Sims is a Kansas City based poet. His desire is to make beautiful art that captures the imagination of his reader. Painting pictures of joy, sorrow and everything inbetween. Poetry is the language of his soul. Helping him better understand himself, and others.

Victor Smith was born to bet everything on the red strokes, to sleep with old whores and good dogs, to wash in park fountains and eat with tame pigeons, to wait for love in the wrong places. Like a bird on the ground, like rats, he knew better than to gather together with others like him in plain sight, in daylight.
He knew that the muse was a cat with green eyes.
He knew, with rain in our shoes, we can all walk on water.
He knew that some poets are born to burn down Oz from the inside.
He knew that death also has green eyes and he offered his throat to the bitch, anyway.

Brandon Whitehead is originally from Oklahoma, where there are generally only two accepted ways in which a man may express himself: silence or rage. Brandon studied violin at the University of Kansas. Yes. Violin. Brandon likes to drink beer, smoke cigarettes and play role-playing games. Brandon has been a furniture mover, a short-order cook, a movie and music reviewer, a bartender, a camera operator for a local news station, a warehouse foreman for a blood bank and a currier of bio-hazardous materials.
Brandon is one of the last of the old-time projectionists.
Brandon has a really cool collection of robot and spaceship toys which you are not allowed to touch. He lives in KC,KS, in a tiny apartment that doesn't adhere to normal Euclidian geometry.
He spends his nights writing poems and stories while listening to the strange, silent old man that lives above him play the violin.

www.ingramcontent.com/pod-product-compliance
Lightning Source LLC
Chambersburg PA
CBHW021450080526
44588CB00009B/772